todd huisken

BIBLE

ORIGAMI

Other books by Todd Huisken
Mormon Origami
More Mormon Origami

todd huisken

BIBLE ORIGAMI

Plain Sight Publishing
An Imprint of Cedar Fort, Inc.
SPRINGVILLE, UTAH

978-1-4621-1960-8

Published by Plain Sight Publishing, an imprint of Cedar Fort, Inc.
2373 W. 700 S., Springville, UT 84663
Distributed by Cedar Fort, Inc., www.cedarfort.com

Library of Congress Control Number: 2016952191

Cover design by Jon Black and Shawnda T. Craig
Interior layout design by Shawnda T. Craig
Cover design © 2016 Cedar Fort, Inc.
Edited by Chelsea Holdaway

Printed in United States of America

10 9 8 7 6 5 4 3 2 1

To my beautiful wife, Jill, who also happens to
be my best friend. And to Kylie, Jolie, Sophie,
and Dean who have taught me where joy
and happiness come from in life.

CONTENTS

INTRODUCTION
to origami

Origami (pronounced or-i-GA-me) is a Japanese word that means "to fold paper" and is known as the Japanese art of folding paper into shapes representing objects. Paper folding has been practiced for thousands of years, first beginning between AD 100-200 in China. But even though origami began in China, it didn't become widely popular until the Japanese took a liking to it in AD 600.

In the beginning, when paper was first invented and was expensive, origami was used for religious occasions such as weddings and Chinese tea ceremonies. But today, origami can be found in all types of settings, such as schools, churches, art galleries, and museums. If you watch carefully, you can even spot origami figures on television.

You'll notice that each origami design in this book has a skill level listed at the top of the page. Skill level 1 is the easiest, so start there and then work your way up to the skill level 3 designs, which are the most challenging. An index at the back of the book will help you find designs based on skill level.

I hope you enjoy folding the designs in this book, which come from the stories found in the Old Testament and New Testament of the Holy Bible.

ORIGAMI
TERMINOLOGY, SYMBOLS & FOLDS

FOLDS

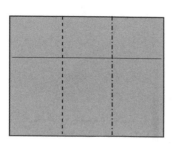 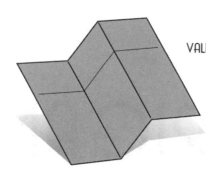

VALLEY FOLDS are represented by a dashed line. MOUNTAIN FOLDS by a dot-dash line.
PRECREASES are shown with a thin line that does not touch the sides:
all FOLDED or RAW EDGES are shown with a thick line.

A RABBIT-EAR is a procedure where four folds are made at once. meeting at a vertex. Generally. you will precrease all three of them. and flatten the fourth into place.

 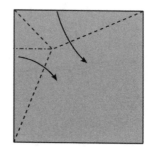 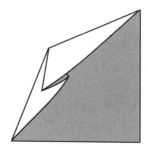

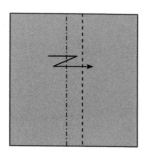 

A PLEAT creates two creases. one mountain & one valley. Usually the mountain is precreased & the valley is flattened into place.

FOLDS

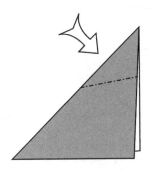
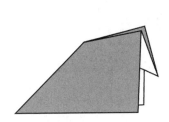

INSIDE REVERSE FOLDS change the direction of the spine
of a flap. adding two creases along the way.

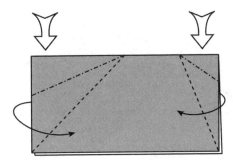
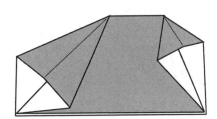

SQUASH FOLDS take the spine of a flap. open it up & flatten it.
Usually the valley crease is precreased.

FOLDS

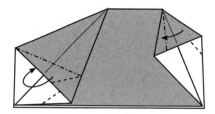 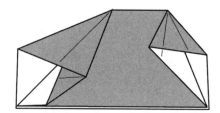

A SWIVEL fold takes an area of paper & pivots it around a vertex.
Swivel folds fall into the same group of operations as squash & reverse folds.

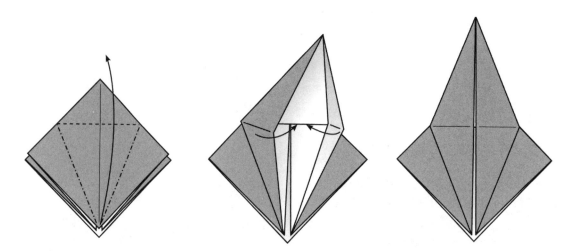

A PETAL fold is like doing two squash folds at once.
This is difficult. so try to precrease as much of it as possible first.

OLD TESTAMENT
DESIGNS

SERPENT

DID YOU KNOW?
In the Bible, the serpent is used as a symbol of both Jesus Christ (Numbers 21:5-9) and Satan (Genesis 3:1-6).

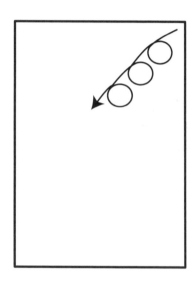

1. Begin with a rectangular piece of paper. Tightly roll the paper diagonally toward the opposite corner.

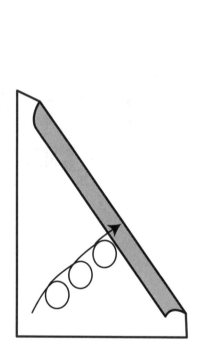

2. As you near the corner, begin rolling the opposite corner toward the roll from step 1. This will help keep the tube from unrolling.

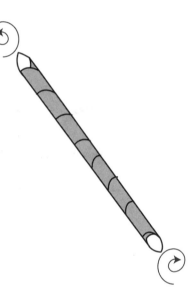

3. Gently twist the tube in opposite directions to tighten.

DID YOU KNOW?
The word "fiery" in "fiery serpents" is used to describe the burning sensation caused by the serpent's bite.

artwork: Nick Robinson
design: Todd Huisken

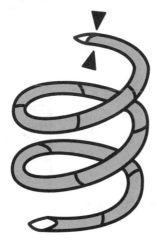

5. Flatten one end of the tube to form serpent head.

4. Carefully twist the tube into a coil shape.

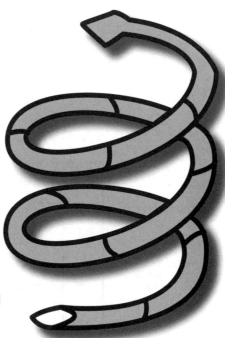

6. Serpent finished!

NOAH'S ARK
Design #1

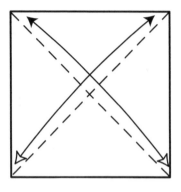

1. Fold in half diagonally both directions and unfold.

Turn model over.

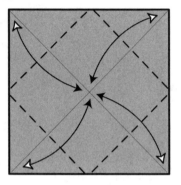

2. Fold four corners to the center and unfold.

Turn model over.

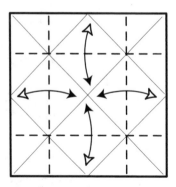

3. Fold four sides to the center and unfold.

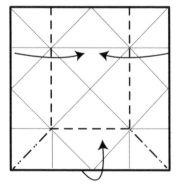

4. Begin to fold the left and right sides to the center. As the sides meet the center, fold the bottom up, allowing the corners to fold outward as shown.

artwork: Nick Robinson
design: Todd Huisken

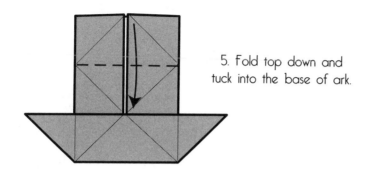

5. Fold top down and tuck into the base of ark.

6. Ark finished!

NOAH'S ARK
Design #2—Hull

DID YOU KNOW?
The ark Noah built was 450 feet long, which is the length of 1 1/4 football fields or about half the length of the Titanic.

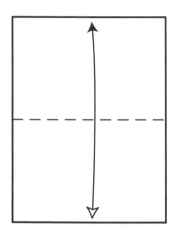

1. Start with an 8.5 x 11 rectangular paper. Fold in half top to bottom and unfold.

2. Fold top and bottom edges to middle and unfold.

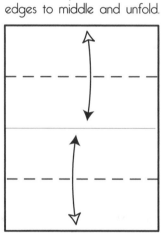

Turn model over.

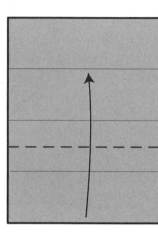

3. Fold bottom edge up to match the upper crease from step 2.

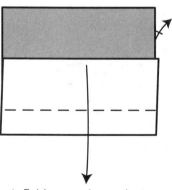

4. Fold upper layer down at lower crease from step 2.

5. Repeat steps 3-4 with top half of model.

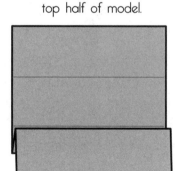

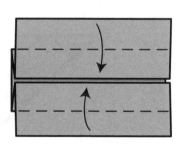

6. Fold top and bottom flaps into middle.

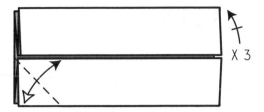

7. Fold bottom left corner in and unfold.
Repeat on remaining three corners.

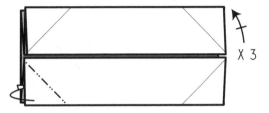

8. Tuck top layer corners inside
the model on all four corners.

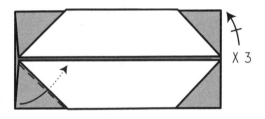

9. Tuck bottom layer corners inside
the model on all four corners.

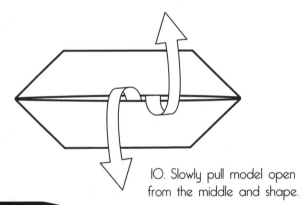

10. Slowly pull model open
from the middle and shape.

11. Hull finished!

NOAH'S ARK
Design #2—Deck

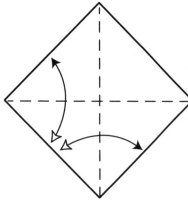

1. Start with a 4.5 x 4.5 square paper. Fold in half diagonally side to side and unfold.

2. Fold in bottom left side where shown.

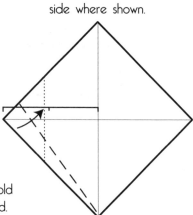

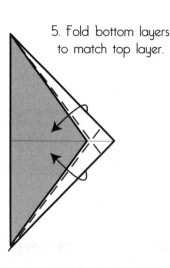

3. Fold in upper left side where shown.

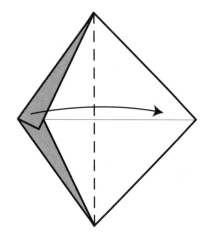

4. Fold the left side over to the right side.

5. Fold bottom layers to match top layer.

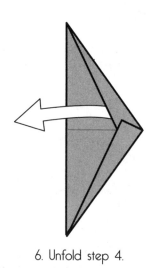

6. Unfold step 4.

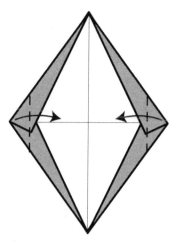

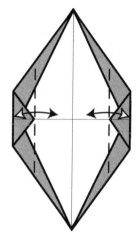

7. Fold sides in where shown.

8. Fold sides back and
forth along the dotted line.

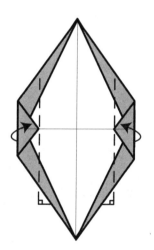

9. Fold sides in at
a right angle.

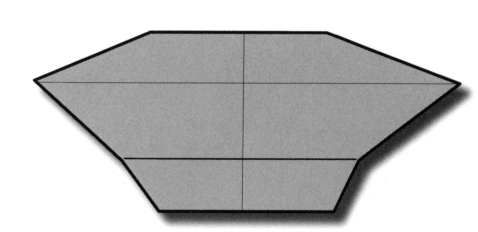

10. Model should look like this.
Deck finished!

NOAH'S ARK
Design #2—Cabin

DID YOU KNOW?
When the Earth was flooded, there was so much water that the ark floated over the tops of mountains.

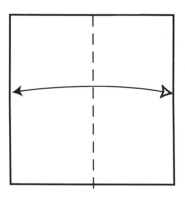

1. Start with a 4.5 x 4.5 square paper. Fold in half side to side and unfold.

2. Fold in half top to bottom.

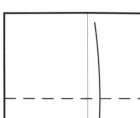

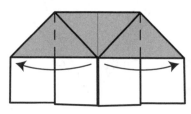

3. Fold sides into center and unfold.

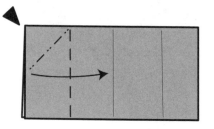

4. While folding the left side to the center, open slightly and squash flap flat.

5. While folding the right side to the center, open slightly and squash flap flat.

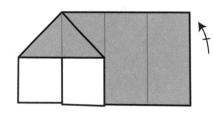

6. Fold the center top layer to the right and left as shown.

DID YOU KNOW?
The ark was so large, researchers estimate it took Noah between 70 and 120 years to build.

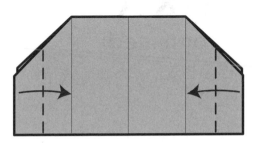

7. Fold the top layer of sides in.

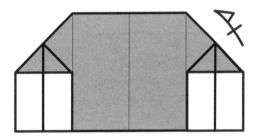

8. Fold the bottom layer of sides back.

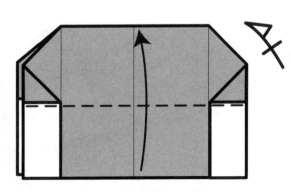

9. Fold the top layer up. Fold the bottom layer back to match the top layer.

NOAH'S ARK
Design #2—Cabin (continued)

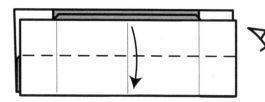

10. Fold the edge of the top layer down. Repeat with the bottom layer on the back of the model. Rotate model 180 degrees.

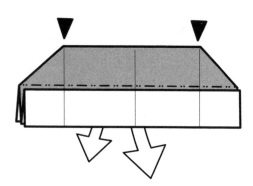

11. Carefully pull the sides apart and form a rectangular box shape. The box will have two flaps.

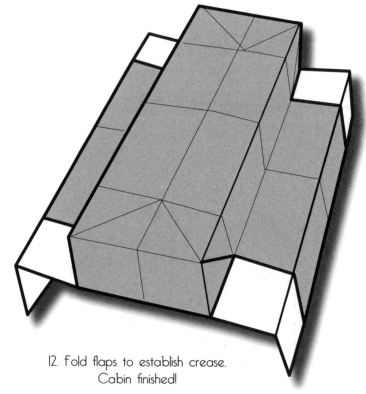

12. Fold flaps to establish crease. Cabin finished!

NOAH'S ARK

Design #2—Assembly

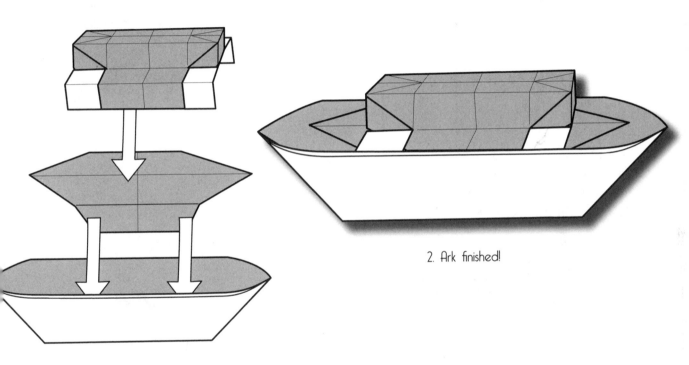

2. Ark finished!

1. Insert tabs of the deck in between the layer
on the side of the hull. Bend ends of deck to fit.
Insert flaps from cabin in between the layers of
the side of the hull. Cabin will sit on the deck.
Deck will sit on the hull.

DID YOU KNOW?

Foxes have whiskers on their legs as well as around their faces, which they use to help them navigate.

FOX
Ark Animal

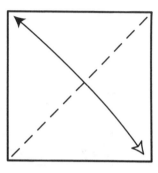

1. Start with a square paper. Fold in half diagonally from the bottom right corner up to the top left corner and unfold.

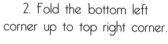

2. Fold the bottom left corner up to top right corner.

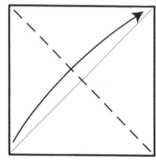

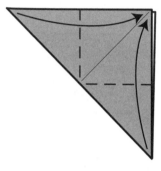

3. Fold the two corners up to the top right point.

Turn model over.

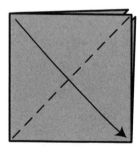

4. Fold in half diagonally from the top left corner down to the bottom right corner.

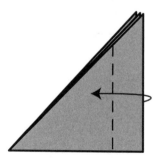

5. Fold right side over to left.

DID YOU KNOW?
A male fox is called a "dog" while a female fox is called a "vixen."

artwork: Nick Robinson
design: Todd Huisken

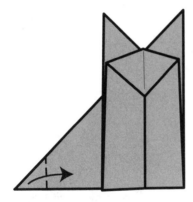

6. Fold four of the layers from step 5 back to the right, pushing the middle point down to form the face. Flatten the points on either side to form the ears.

7. Fold the bottom left point over to form the tail.

8. Fox finished!

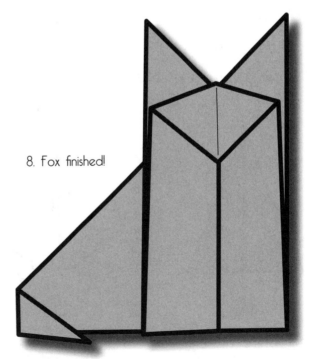

DID YOU KNOW?
Sperm whales can swallow
whole seals and giant squids.

Jonah and
THE WHALE

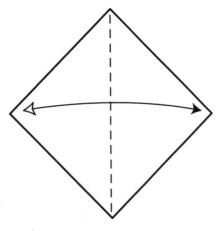

1. Start with a square paper. Fold in
   half diagonally and unfold.

2. Fold sides into the middle.

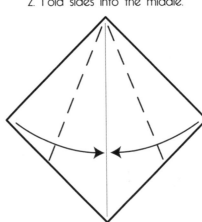

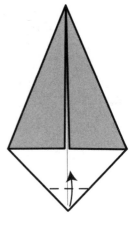

3. Fold bottom point up.

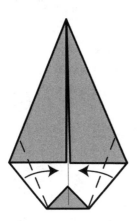

4. Fold sides as shown.

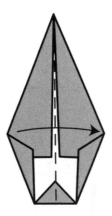

5. Fold in half.

Rotate model 90 degrees.

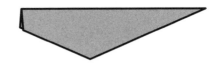

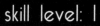
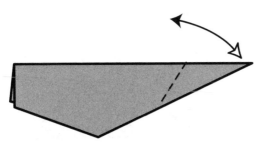

6. Fold left point back and forth to prepare for step 7.

DID YOU KNOW?
Jesus compared Jonah's experience to His own death and resurrection. pointing out the miraculous nature of both (Matthew 12:40).

artwork: Nick Robinson
design: Todd Huisken

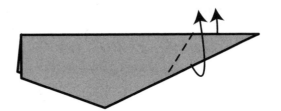

7. Open model slightly and fold point up.

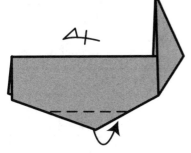

8. Fold bottom points up to create flippers.

9. Whale finished!

Daniel and the Lion's Den
LION

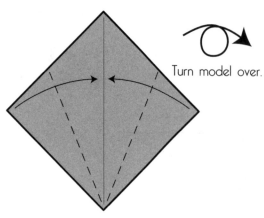

Turn model over.

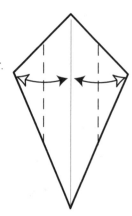

Turn model over.

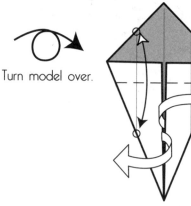

1. Start with a square paper. Fold left and right corners into the middle.

2. Fold sides into the middle and unfold. Turn model over.

3. Fold bottom up along the dotted line, matching the points shown. Then unfold model completely.

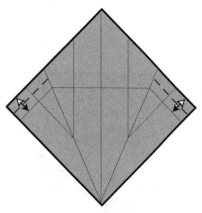

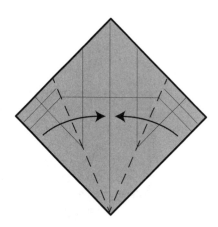

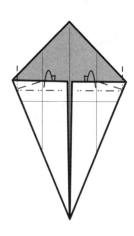

4. Fold and unfold sides to form crease where shown.

5. Fold sides into the middle.

6. Fold flaps from step 4 inside model.

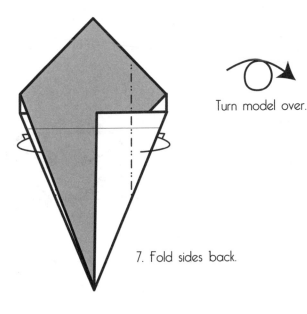

Turn model over.

7. Fold sides back.

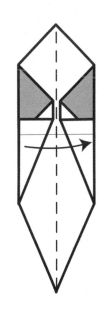

8. Fold model in
half long ways.

Rotate model
90 degrees.

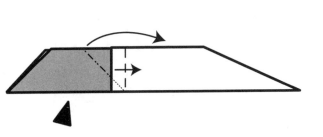

9. Fold left side up and to the right.
Open flap and squash flap flat.

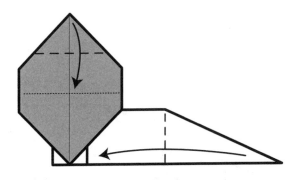

10. Fold top point down.
Fold right point to the left.

Daniel and the Lion's Den
LION (continued)

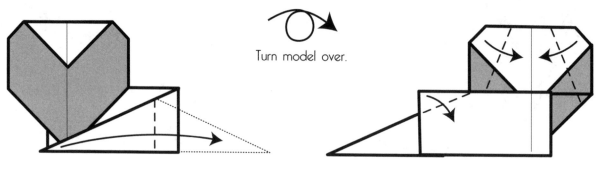

Turn model over.

11. Fold top layer back to the left.

12. Fold three points in as shown.

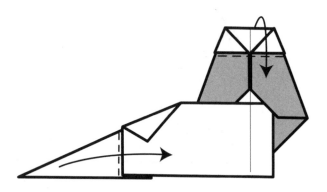

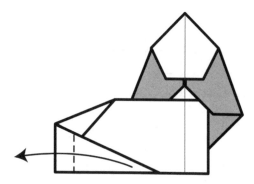

13. Fold top up from other side and bring the front flap down. Fold left point over to the right.

14. Fold top layer back to left along dotted line.

DID YOU KNOW?
A lion can run for short distances at fifty mph and leap as far as thirty-six feet.

artwork & design:
Nick Robinson

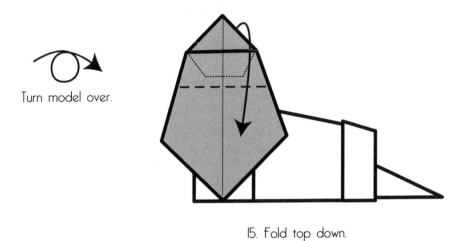

Turn model over.

15. Fold top down.

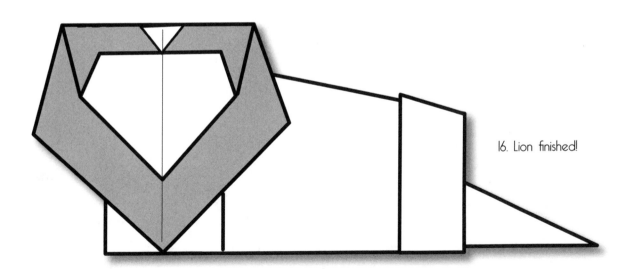

16. Lion finished!

TOWER of Babel

TOP LAYER

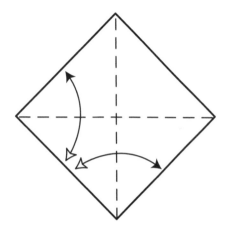

1. Start with a square paper. Fold in half diagonally both ways and unfold.

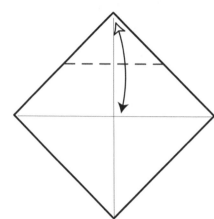

2. Fold top corner to center then unfold.

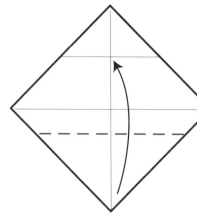

3. Fold bottom corner up to the crease made in step 2.

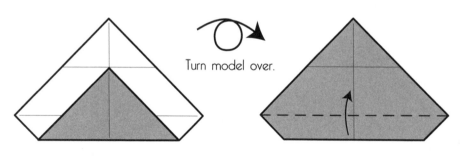

Turn model over.

4. Fold flap up.

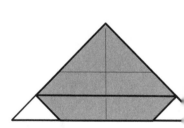

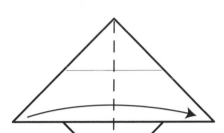

urn model over.

5. Unfold the small triangle.

6. Fold in half left to right.

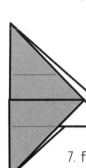

7. First half is finished. With a new piece of paper, repeat steps 1-6.

nk the two halves together by sliding "arms" of the units into each other.

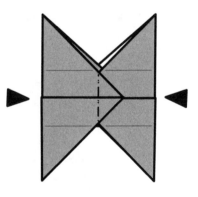

9. Push the two halves together, making sure they do not come apart. Open the model and fold in half, matching the image in step 10.

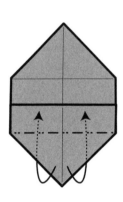

10. Fold the lower points up inside the model to lock them in place. Shape the model so that the base is in the shape of a square.

TOWER of Babel
(continued)

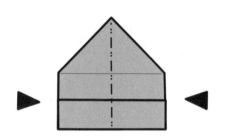

11. Open the model, refolding it to match the image in step 12.

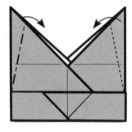

12. Fold the point on the right toward the front and fold the point on the left toward the back.

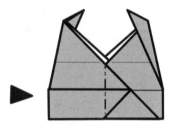

13. Push the sides together, opening the model.

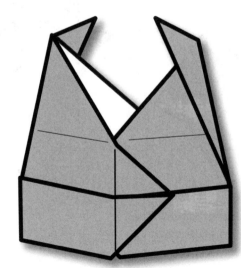

14. Top layer finished!

BOTTOM LAYER

skill level: 2

DID YOU KNOW?
Work on the Tower of Babel stopped after God confounded the people's language and scattered the people.

artwork: Nick Robinson
design: Todd Huisken

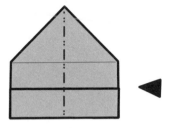

1. Repeat steps 1-11 of the Tower of Babel top layer.

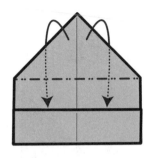

2. Fold the top points inside the model.

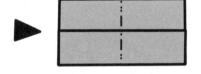

3. Push the sides together.

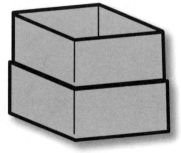

4. Bottom layer finished! Repeat for more layers.

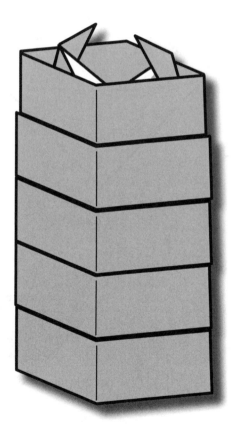

Layers may be stacked on top of each other by fitting the top of one layer inside the bottom of another. Stack layers as high as you want your tower to be.

5. Tower finished!

BURNING BUSH

FLAMES PART I

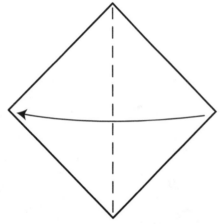

1. Start with a square paper. Fold in half diagonally right to left.

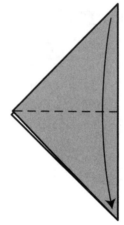

2. Fold in half top to bottom.

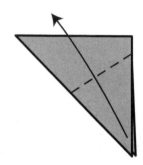

3. Fold top layer at dotted line. (Note: line is not centered.)

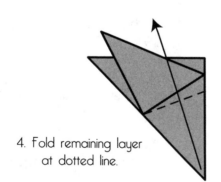

4. Fold remaining layer at dotted line.

5. Part I finished!

FLAMES PART 2

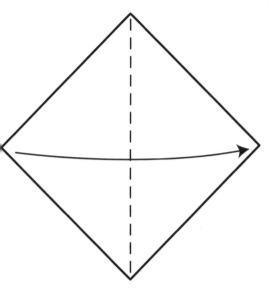

1. Start with a square paper. Fold in half diagonally left to right.

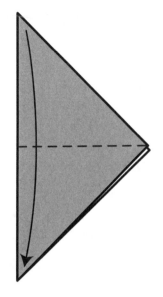

2. Fold in half top to bottom.

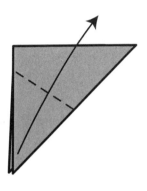

3. Fold top layer at dotted line. (Note: line is not centered.)

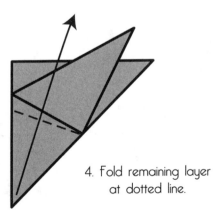

4. Fold remaining layer at dotted line.

5. Part 2 finished!

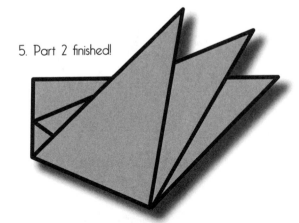

DID YOU KNOW?
Though no one knows for sure, some Jewish scholars believe that the burning bush may have been a type of thorny acacia bush.

BURNING BUSH
(continued)

FLAMES ASSEMBLY

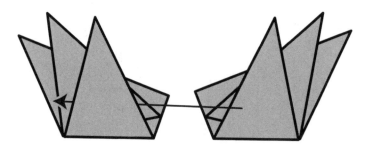

1. Slide part 2 behind the first layer of part 1.

2. Tuck in flap to lock model. Bend and twist flames to shape.

3. Flames finished!

BUSH

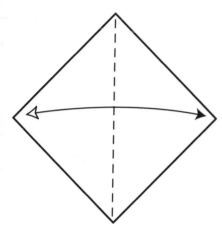

1. Start with a square paper. Fold in half diagonally side to side and unfold.

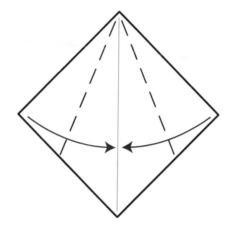

2. Fold sides to center.

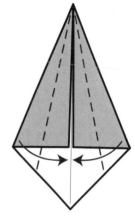

3. Fold sides to center again.

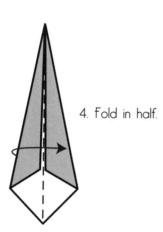

4. Fold in half.

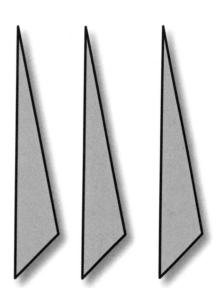

5. Repeat steps 1-4 to make a total of three branches.

BURNING BUSH
(continued)

BUSH PART 1

1. Fold and unfold to make crease.

2. Open model slightly and fold sides back.

3. Part 1 finished.

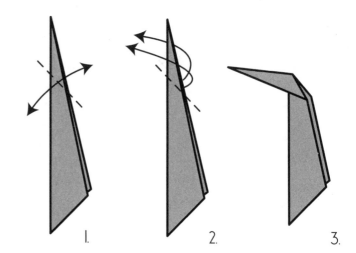

1.   2.   3.

BUSH PART 2

1. Fold and unfold to make crease.

2. Fold sides back to make inside reverse fold.

3. Part 2 finished.

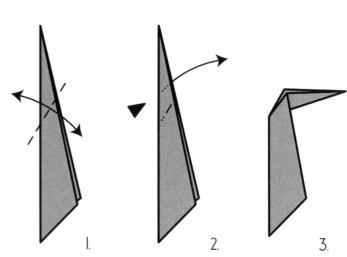

1.   2.   3.

BUSH ASSEMBLY

artwork: Nick Robinson
design: Todd Huisken

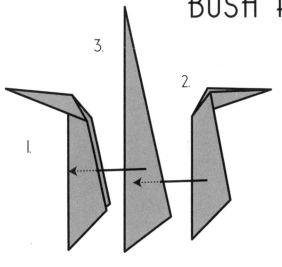

3.

2.

1.

2. Fold in bottom flap to lock model.

1. Layer three bush parts inside one another in order of 1, 3, 2.

3. Make a pleat on the base of the model to allow it to stand up and hold the flames.

4. Insert flames behind bush. Pleated part of base should support flames.

5. Burning bush finished!

Joseph's COAT
of Many Colors

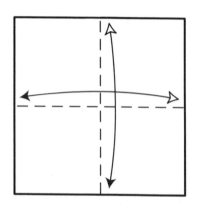

1. Start with a square paper. Fold in half top to bottom and side to side. Unfold.

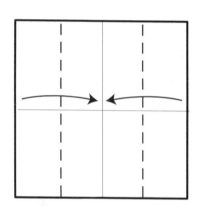

2. Fold sides into middle.

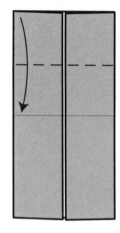

3. Fold top down to middle.

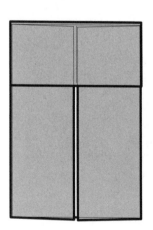

Turn model over.

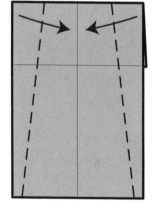

4. Fold sides following the dotted line.

DID YOU KNOW?
Some bible scholars believe that the Hebrew description of Joseph's coat indicates that it was a "long coat with sleeves" and not a "colorful" coat.

artwork: Nick Robinson
design: Todd Huisken

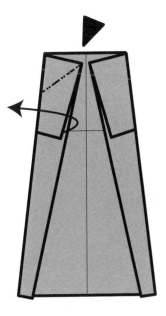

5. Open top left flap slightly and squash flap flat.

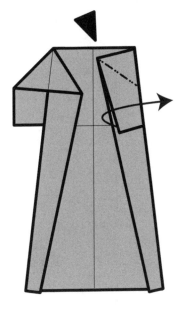

6. Open top right flap slightly and squash flap flat.

7. Coat finished!

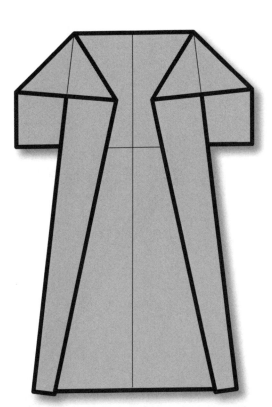

Moses's STAFF
with Serpent

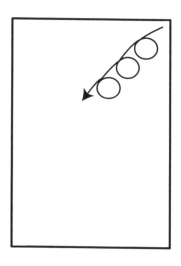

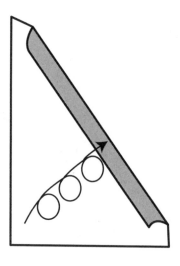

1. Begin with a rectangular piece of paper. Tightly roll the paper diagonally toward the opposite corner.

2. As you near the corner. begin rolling the opposite corner toward the roll from step 1. This will help keep the tube from unrolling.

3. Gently twist the tube in opposite directions to tighten.

DID YOU KNOW?
The children of Israel only had to look at Moses's staff with the serpent on it in order to be healed from poisonous snakebites (Numbers 21:7-9).

artwork: Nick Robinson
design: Todd Huisken

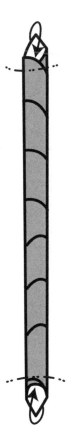

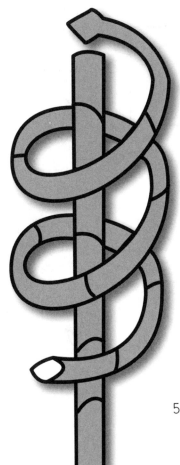

4. Tuck ends inside the tube to lock into place. Carefully wrap serpent model (from pages 8 and 9) around staff.

5. Staff finished!

MANNA

DID YOU KNOW?
The book of Exodus tells us
that raw manna tasted like
wafers made with honey
(Exodus 16:31).

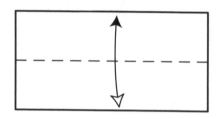

1. Begin with a rectangular paper. Fold
in half top to bottom and unfold.

2. Fold left corners in and unfold to
create creases only where shown.
Repeat on right side.

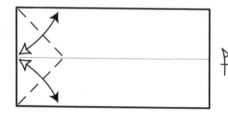

3. Fold in half right to left.

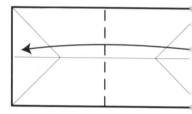

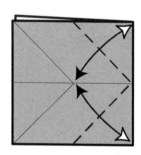

4. Fold right corners back and
forth to prepare for step 5.

Rotate model left
90 degrees.

5. Open model slightly
and tuck corners in.

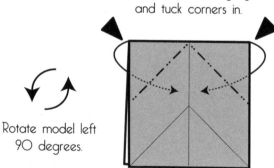

6. Fold top back and forth
to establish crease.

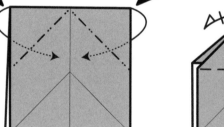

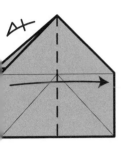

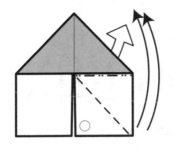

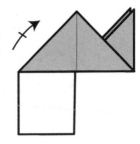

DID YOU KNOW?
Manna had to be collected before it was melted by the sun (Exodus 16:21).

artwork: Nick Robinson
design: Todd Huisken

7. Fold top layer to the right. Fold the back right layer behind to the left.

8. Open right side slightly. Hold bottom left corner and push up into the larger fold.

9. Repeat on left side.

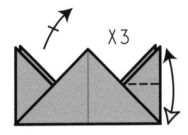

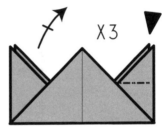

10. Fold and unfold top point to establish crease. Repeat on remaining three points.

11. Open model slightly and tuck in point. Repeat on remaining three points.

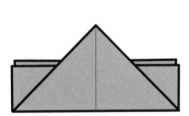

12. Allow model to open.

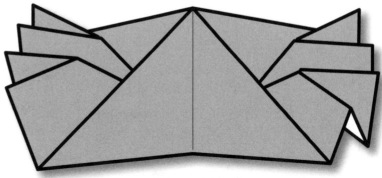

13. Manna finished!

ARK of the COVENANT

BOX

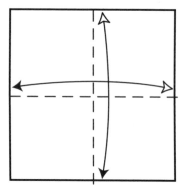

1. Start with a square paper. Fold in half top to bottom and side to side. Unfold.

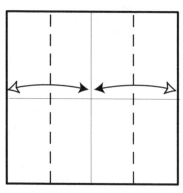

2. Fold sides into middle and unfold.

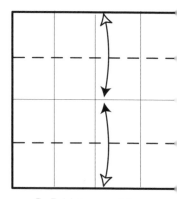

3. Fold top and bottom to middle and unfold.

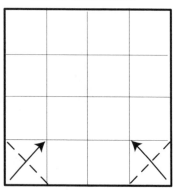

4. Fold bottom corners up.

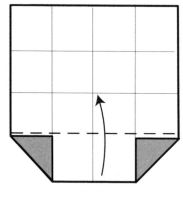

5. Fold bottom up.

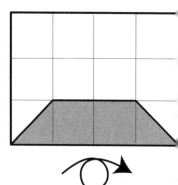

Turn model over.

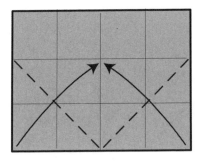

6. Fold bottom corners up.

7. Fold top corners down.

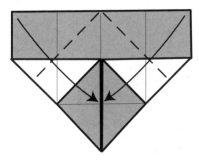

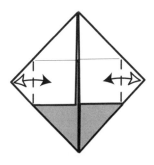

8. Fold sides back and forth to establish crease.

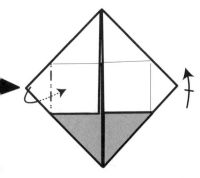

9. Open model slightly and squash side corners in.

10. Unfold top.

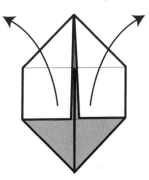

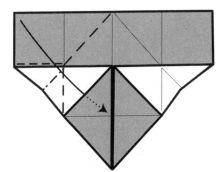

11. Pinch top left corner and push left pocket open. Tuck corner into left pocket.

ARK of the COVENANT

BOX (continued)

12. Pinch top right corner and push the right pocket open. Tuck corner into right pocket.

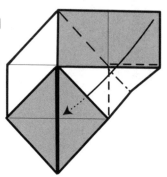

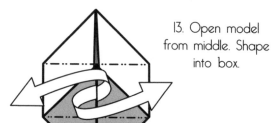

13. Open model from middle. Shape into box.

14. Box finished!

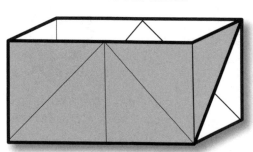

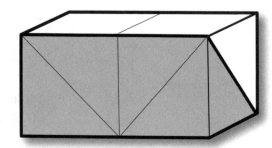

ARK of the COVENANT

SERAPHIM

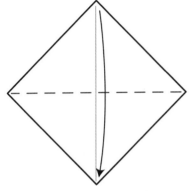

1. Begin with a square piece of paper 1/4 the size of the one used for the ark box. Fold in half diagonally top to bottom.

2. Fold in half side to side and unfold.

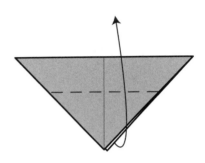

3. Fold bottom up as shown.

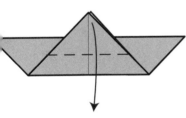

4. Fold top layer down.

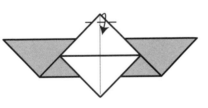

5. Fold point down.

7. First seraphim finished! With a new piece of paper, repeat steps 1-6 to make the second seraphim.

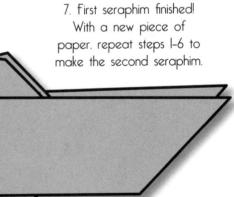

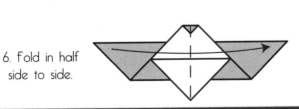

6. Fold in half side to side.

DID YOU KNOW?
The ark was fifty-two inches long, thirty-one inches wide, and thirty-one inches high.

ARK of the COVENANT

POLES

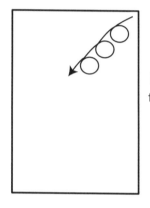

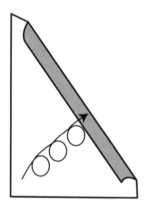

1. Begin with a rectangular paper half the size of the paper used for the ark box. Tightly roll the paper diagonally toward the opposite corner.

2. As you near the corner, begin rolling opposite corner toward the roll from step 1. This will help keep the tube from unrolling.

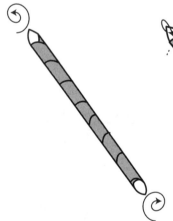

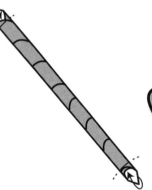

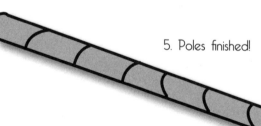

5. Poles finished!

3. Gently twist the tube in opposite directions to tighten.

4. Tuck in ends to lock tube. Repeat steps 1-4 with a new piece of paper to create second pole.

ARK of the COVENANT
ASSEMBLY
(Requires cutting)

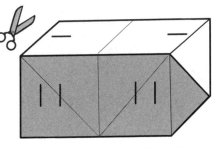

1. Cut two slits on top of the box. Cut four slits on both of the long sides of the box.

2. Insert seraphim into slits on top of the box. Slide poles into slits on both sides of the box.

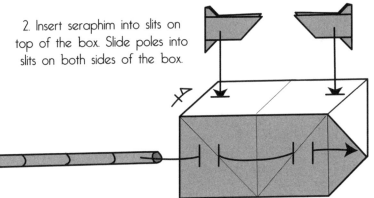

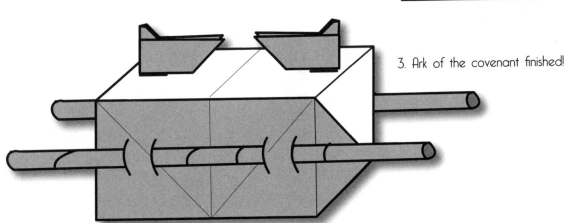

3. Ark of the covenant finished!

Ten Commandments
TABLETS

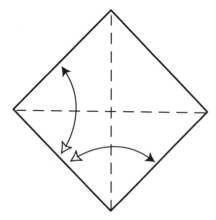

1. Fold in half diagonally both ways and unfold.

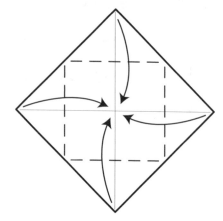

2. Fold four corners into middle.

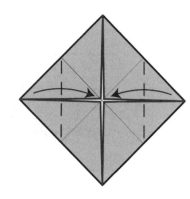

3. Fold sides into middle.

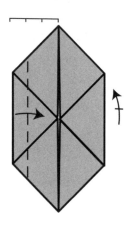

4. Fold sides in as shown.

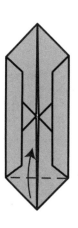

5. Fold bottom point up.

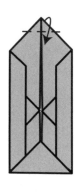

6. Fold top point down.

DID YOU KNOW?

According to some traditions, the words on the stone tablets were not engraved on the surface, but rather were bored fully through the stone.

artwork: Nick Robinson
design: Todd Huisken

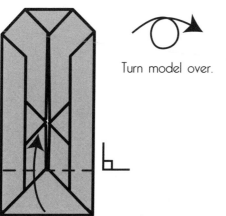

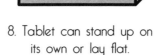

Turn model over.

7. Fold bottom up where shown.

8. Tablet can stand up on its own or lay flat.

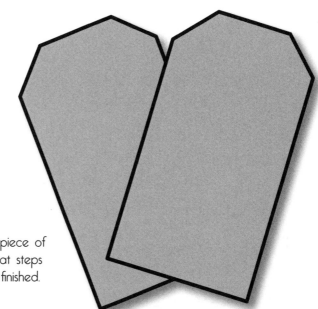

9. With new piece of paper, repeat steps 1-8. Tablets finished.

NEW TESTAMENT

─ DESIGNS ─

STAR of Bethlehem
(Requires cutting)

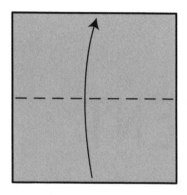

1. Start with a square paper. Fold paper in half bottom to top.

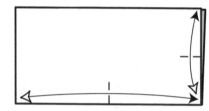

2. Fold in half left to right and top to bottom to establish small creases where shown, in preparation for step 3.

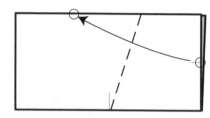

3. Fold right side to the left as shown, using the creases from step 2.

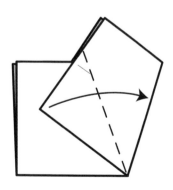

4. Fold upper layer to right.

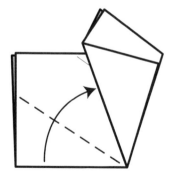

5. Fold bottom left corner up to meet folded right side.

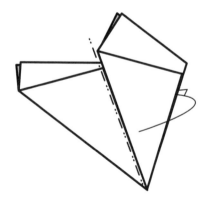

6. Fold right side behind.

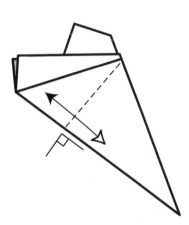

7. Fold back and forth where shown to establish crease.

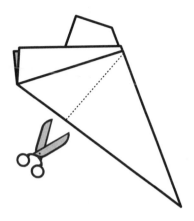

8. Cut all layers at crease from step 7. Unfold model.

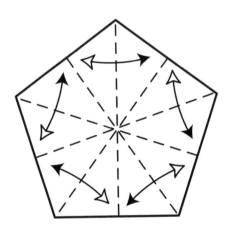

9. Fold and unfold five time to flatten creases where shown.

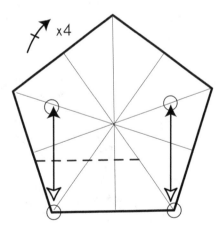

10. Fold bottom up, matching the points, and only creasing where shown. Repeat on remaining four sides.

STAR of Bethlehem
(continued)

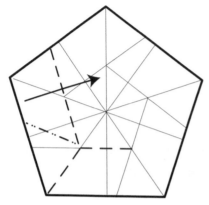

11. Fold side in and bottom up and unfold as shown to establish creases.

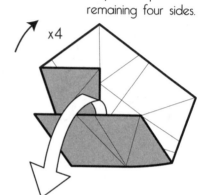

12. Repeat step 11 on the remaining four sides.

x4

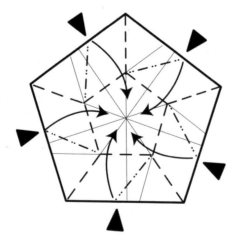

13. Slowly and carefully fold each of the five sides to the middle at the same time. They will lie down in a flat star shape.

DID YOU KNOW?
The Star of Bethlehem is traditionally linked to the prophecy in the book of Numbers (Numbers 24:17).

artwork: Nick Robinson
design: Todd Huisken

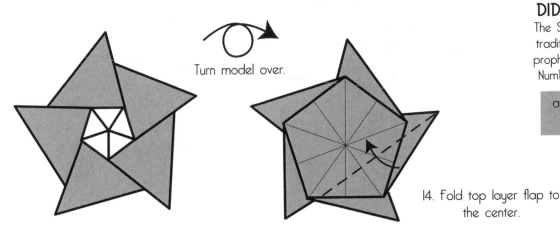

Turn model over.

14. Fold top layer flap to the center.

16. Star finished.

15. Fold the flap to the left of step 14 to the middle. Repeat with remaining three flaps, moving clockwise.

Peter's
FISHING BOAT

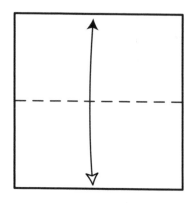

1. Start with a square paper. Fold in half top to bottom and unfold.

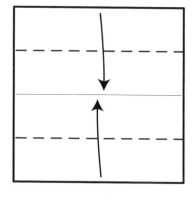

2. Fold the top and bottom edges into the middle.

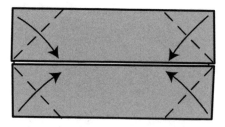

3. Fold all four corners into the middle.

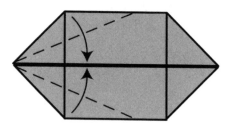

4. Fold left edges in.

DID YOU KNOW?

In 1986, two fishermen brothers, Moshe and Yuval Lufan, discovered an ancient boat buried in the mud in the Sea of Galilee that dated back to the time of Jesus and His apostles.

artwork: Nick Robinson
design: Todd Huisken

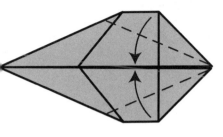

5. Fold right edges in.

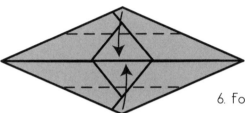

6. Fold the top and bottom points into the middle.

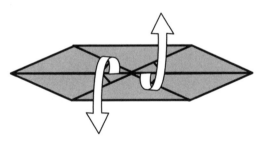

7. Push up on the bottom of the model and carefully turn the model inside out.

Turn model over.

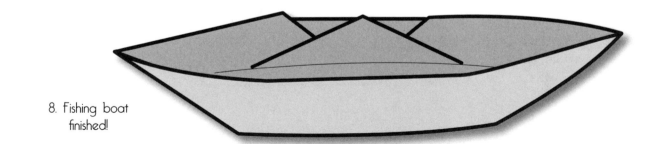

8. Fishing boat finished!

SHEPHERD'S CROOK

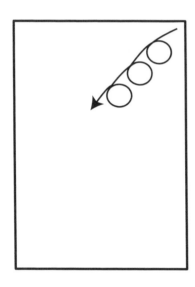

1. Begin with a rectangular piece of paper. Tightly roll the paper diagonally toward the opposite corner.

2. As you near the corner, begin rolling the opposite corner toward the roll from step 1. This will help keep the tube from unrolling.

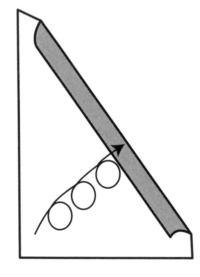

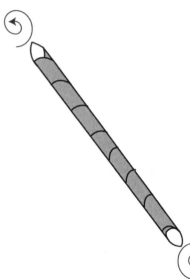

3. Gently twist the tube in opposite directions to tighten.

DID YOU KNOW?

Besides herding sheep, the shepherd's crook was also used for balancing, examining dangerous undergrowth, and defending against wild animal attacks.

artwork: Nick Robinson
design: Todd Huisken

5. Carefully bend end of tube into a curved shape.

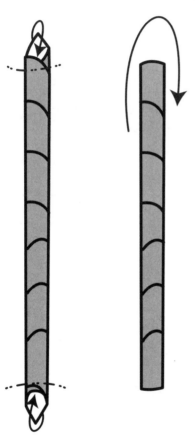

4. Tuck in the ends to lock tube.

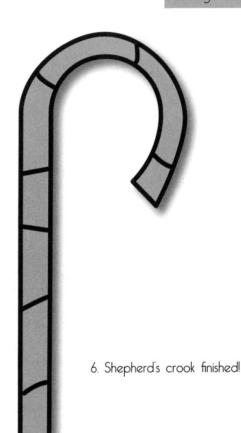

6. Shepherd's crook finished!

SHEEP

DID YOU KNOW?
Sheep are thoroughly familiar with their own shepherd's voice and would follow the voice of their shepherd.

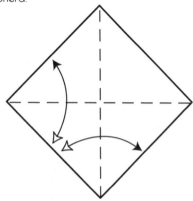

1. Start with a square paper. Fold in half diagonally top to bottom, and side to side. Unfold.

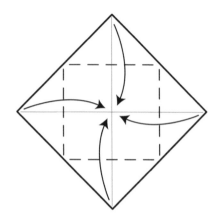

2. Fold four corners into the middle.

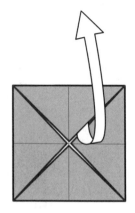

3. Fold top layer up.

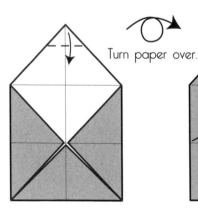

Turn paper over.

4. Fold top point down.

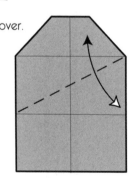

5. Fold top left corner down and unfold as shown.

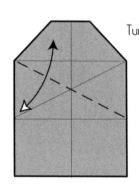

6. Fold top right corner down and unfold as shown.

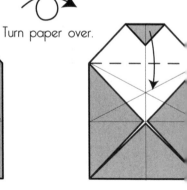

Turn paper over.

7. Fold top dow

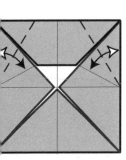

Fold corners back and
rth to establish creases.

Rotate model
90 degrees

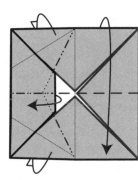

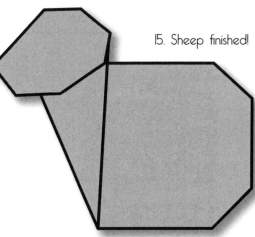

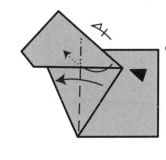

DID YOU KNOW?

A sheep can produce
anywhere from two to thirty
pounds of wool a year.

artwork & design:
Nick Robinson

9. While slowly folding the top down and in
half, push the left side of the paper back
allowing it to fold using the creases from
steps 5 and 6. The left side of model will
pull back to form the head of the sheep.

10. Fold flaps on top layer
back and forth. Open the
top layer and tuck flap inside.
Repeat on back of model.

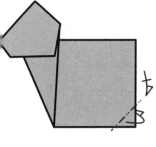

11. Fold in the bottom right corner
on upper and lower layer.

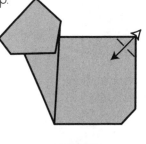

12. Fold the top right
corner back and forth.

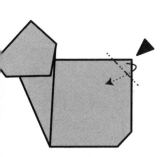

3. Open model slightly and
push in top right corner.

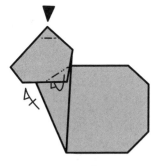

14. Fold the point on top of head back
and forth, then tuck into the top of the
head. Fold corner underneath head.
Repeat on back of model.

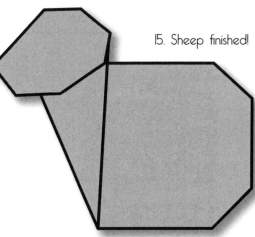

15. Sheep finished!

DID YOU KNOW?
The three types of coins mentioned in the Bible are the widow's mite, the tribute penny, and the thirty pieces of silver.

Parable of the
LOST COIN

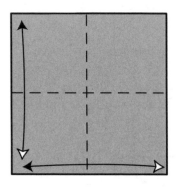

1. Start with a square paper. Fold paper in half side to side and top to bottom. Unfold model.

2. Fold in half diagonally both ways and unfold.

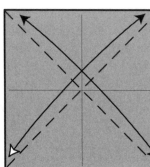

3. Fold all four corners into center and unfold.

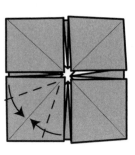

Turn model over.

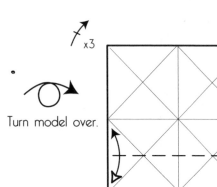

4. Fold bottom up to middle and unfold. Repeat with top, left, and right edges.

5. Slowly fold all four edges toward the center. As the corners come up, gently flatten them so that the corners all meet at the center of the paper.

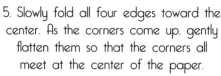

6. In one of the small squares, fold the top layers into the center

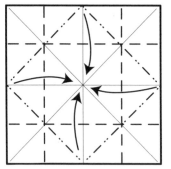

DID YOU KNOW?
Since coins were produced by kings and rulers, the coins often had their images on them.

artwork & design:
Nick Robinson

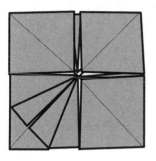

Step 6 completed.

7. In the folded square, fold and unfold a corner of the small triangle to establish crease.

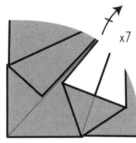

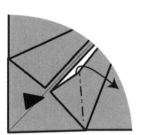

8. Open flap from step 7 and squash flap flat.

x7

9. Repeat steps 6-8 for the remaining 7 sections.

11. Coin finished!

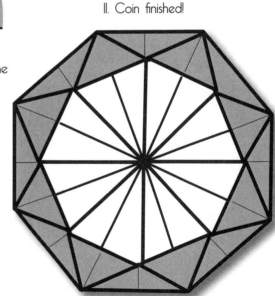

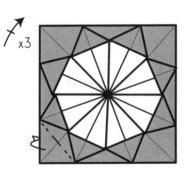

x3

10. Fold bottom left corner back. Repeat with remaining three corners.

FISHES and LOAVES

FISH

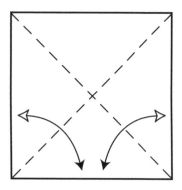

1. Start with a square paper. Fold in half diagonally both ways. Unfold model.

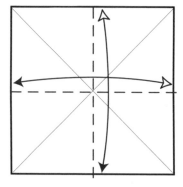

2. Fold in half top to bottom and side to side. Unfold model.

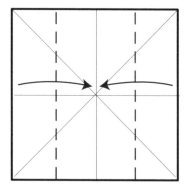

3. Fold sides to middle.

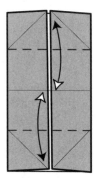

4. Fold top and bottom to middle and unfold.

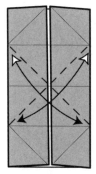

5. Fold and unfold center section where shown to create creases.

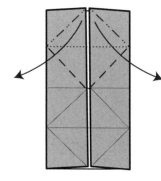

6. Pull top left and right flaps down and out to sides and squash flap flat.

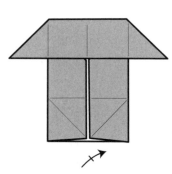

7. Repeat step 6 with flaps on bottom of the model.

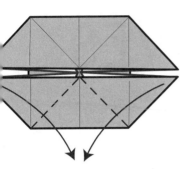

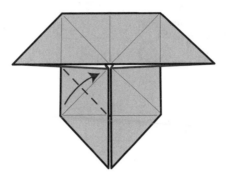

skill level: 1

DID YOU KNOW?

The three main types of fish in the Sea of Galilee at the time of Christ were Musht, Biny, and a type of sardine.

artwork: Nick Robinson
design: Todd Huisken

8. Fold the bottom left and bottom right points down.

9. Fold the bottom left point up and to the right.

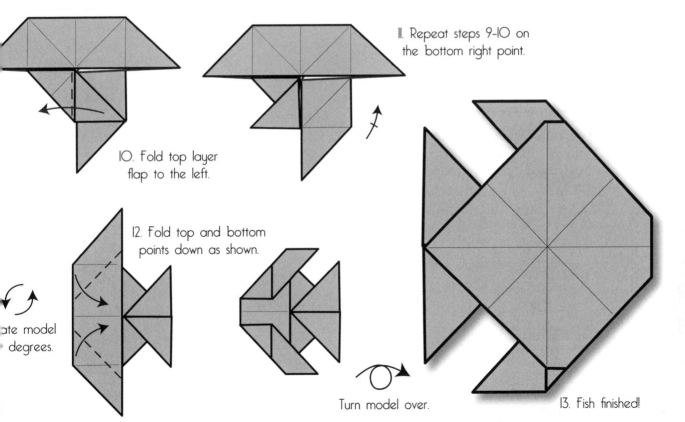

10. Fold top layer flap to the left.

11. Repeat steps 9-10 on the bottom right point.

12. Fold top and bottom points down as shown.

ate model degrees.

Turn model over.

13. Fish finished!

FISHES and LOAVES

DID YOU KNOW?
Most bread in the Bible was baked in either a cone-shaped clay oven called a "tannur" or in the ground in a "pit oven."

BREAD LOAF

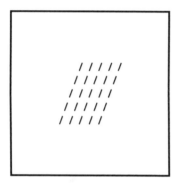

1. Start with a square paper. Make four sharp mountain fold creases where shown. (Note: creases are centered horizontally, but not vertically.)

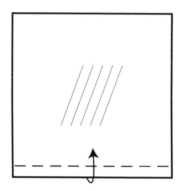

2. Fold bottom edge up.

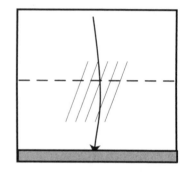

3. Bend (do not fold) upper edge down and tuck into flap created in step 2.

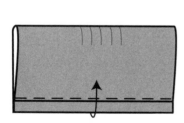

4. Fold lower edge up and crease.

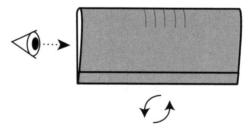

5. Turn model 90 degrees, then turn the model over so the flap is on top.

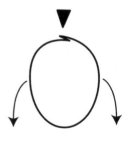

6. Flatten the cylinder making sure the flap is centered.

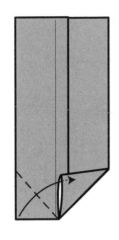
8. Fold left corner in such a way
that you can tuck the edge of
the flap into the flap from step 7.

Fold right corner in.

9. Fold point forward and tuck
inside to lock fold. Rotate model
180 degrees. Insert stuffing (I use
tissue paper), if desired.

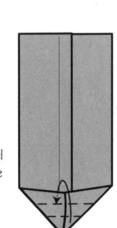

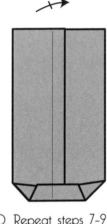

10. Repeat steps 7-9 on
other end of model.

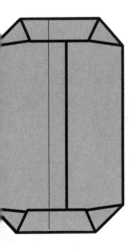

Turn model over.

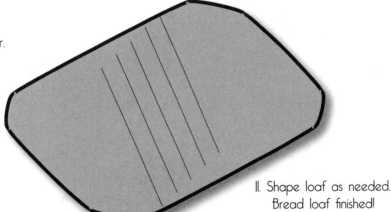

11. Shape loaf as needed.
Bread loaf finished!

DOVE

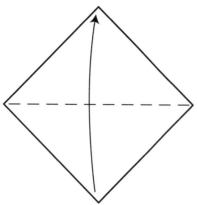

1. Start with a square paper. Fold
in half diagonally bottom to top.

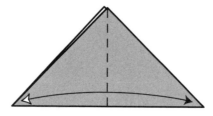

2. Fold in half left to
right and unfold.

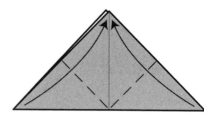

3. Fold corners up.

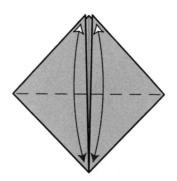

4. Fold top layer points
down and unfold.

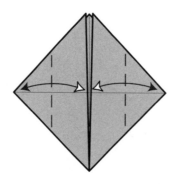

5. Fold sides in to create
crease and unfold.

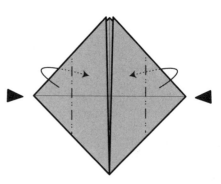

6. Open model slightly, and
push outside points in at
creases from step 5.

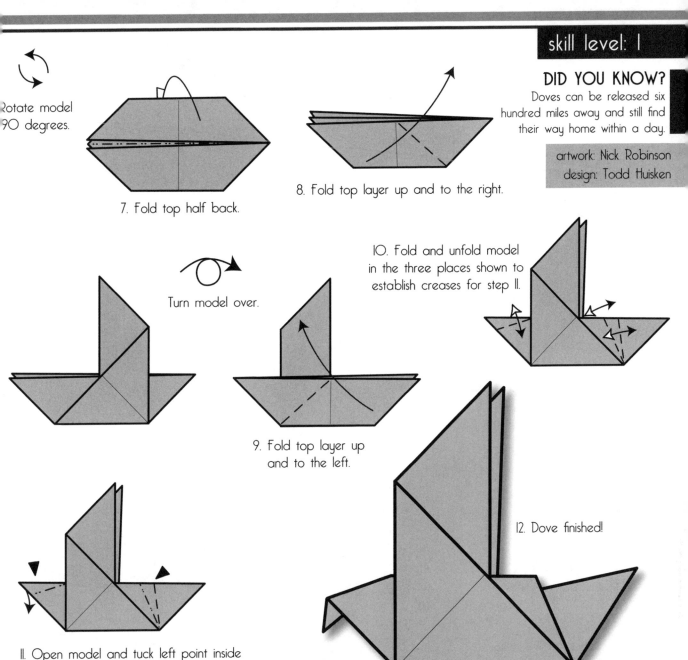

Rotate model 90 degrees.

7. Fold top half back.

8. Fold top layer up and to the right.

skill level: 1

DID YOU KNOW?
Doves can be released six hundred miles away and still find their way home within a day.

artwork: Nick Robinson
design: Todd Huisken

Turn model over.

9. Fold top layer up and to the left.

10. Fold and unfold model in the three places shown to establish creases for step 11.

11. Open model and tuck left point inside as shown. Pleat tail as shown.

12. Dove finished!

OIL LAMP
with Flame

LAMP

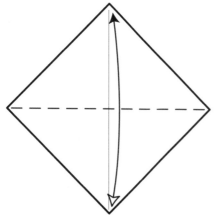

1. Start with a square paper.
Fold in half diagonally top to
bottom. Unfold model.

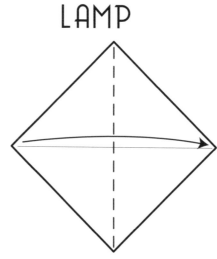

2. Fold in half left to right.

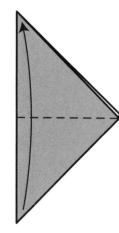

3. Fold in half bottom to top.

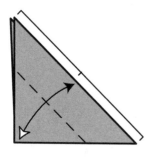

4. Fold corner up. Unfold to
establish crease.

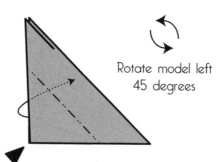

Rotate model left
45 degrees

5. Open model slightly and push point
inside. Squash point flat.

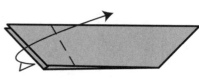

6. Fold both layers of left side
back and forth (at the angle
shown) to establish crease.

DID YOU KNOW?
Some oil lamps were usually made of clay, but the more expensive lamps were made of bronze and sometimes even of gold.

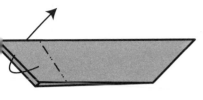

7. Fold top layer inside model.

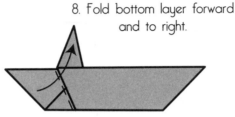

8. Fold bottom layer forward and to right.

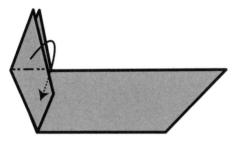

9. Tuck top layer flap inside to lock folds.

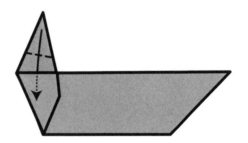

10. Fold point down and tuck inside model.

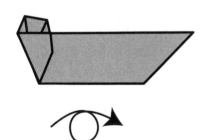

Turn model over.

11. Lamp finished!

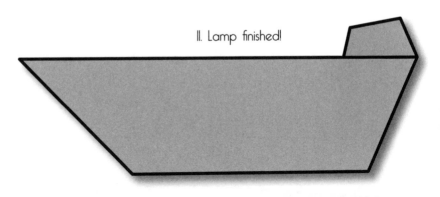

OIL LAMP
with Flame

FLAME

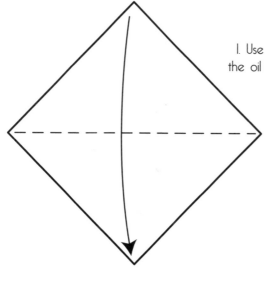

1. Use a square paper 1/4 the size of the oil lamp for best results. Fold in half diagonally top to bottom.

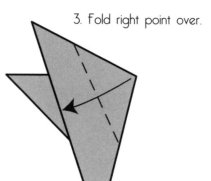

3. Fold right point over.

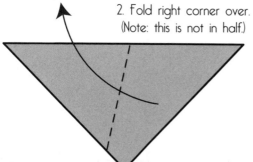

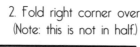

2. Fold right corner over. (Note: this is not in half.)

DID YOU KNOW?
Olive oil was the most common fuel for oil lamps because of the abundance of olive trees in Jerusalem and the surrounding areas.

artwork: Nick Robinson
design: Todd Huisken

Turn model over.

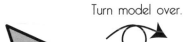

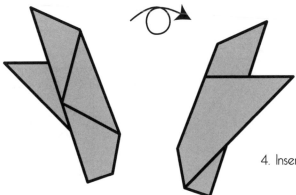

4. Insert flame in end of oil lamp.

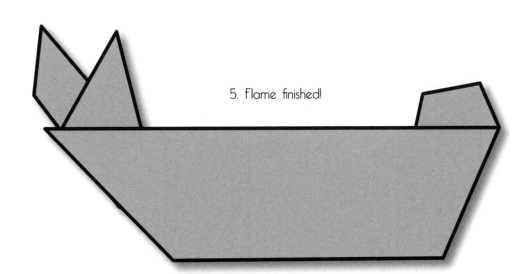

5. Flame finished!

MANGER
and Wrapped Infant

MANGER

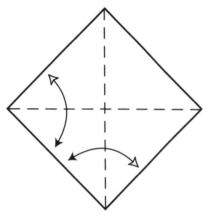

1. Start with a square paper. Fold in half diagonally and unfold.

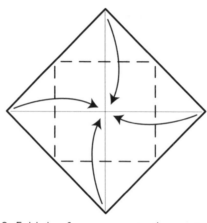

2. Fold the four corners to the center.

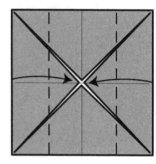

3. Fold sides into the middle.

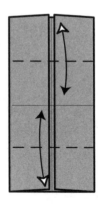

4. Fold top and bottom edges to middle then unfold.

Turn model over.

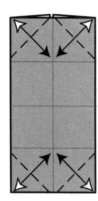

5. Fold four corners back and forth to establish creases.

Turn model over.

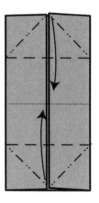

6. Push top layer of top and bottom edges toward the center and allow the corners to fold inward.

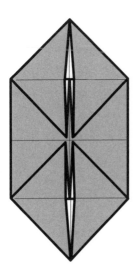

Turn model over.

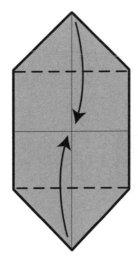

7. Fold top and
bottom flap to middle.

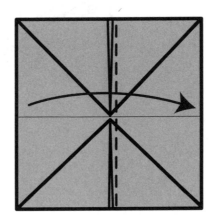

8. Fold in half left to right.

MANGER
and Wrapped Infant
MANGER (continued)

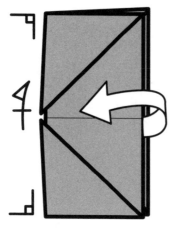

9. Partially unfold step 8 and pull out the
four flaps to create legs for the manger.

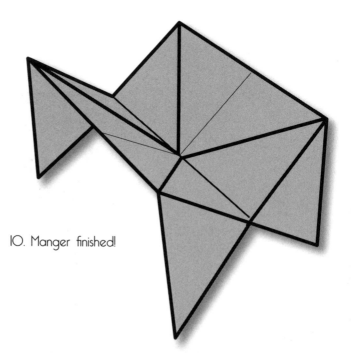

10. Manger finished!

WRAPPED INFANT

skill level: 2

DID YOU KNOW?
Most historians believe that the wise men did not visit Jesus while he was still an infant in the manger, but more likely when he was almost two years old.

artwork: Nick Robinson
design: Todd Huisken

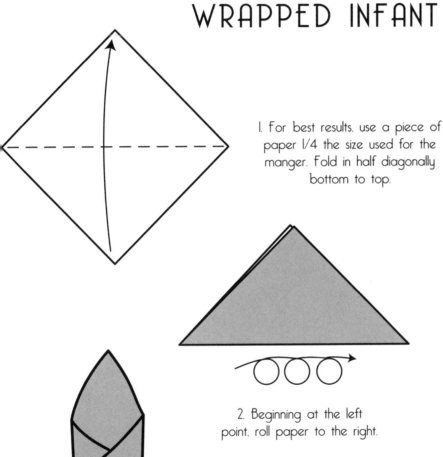

1. For best results, use a piece of paper 1/4 the size used for the manger. Fold in half diagonally bottom to top.

2. Beginning at the left point, roll paper to the right.

3. Shape infant, then fold bottom edge inside and pinch bottom of model to lock in roll. Shape top.

4. Infant finished!

WHEAT
and the Tares

WHEAT

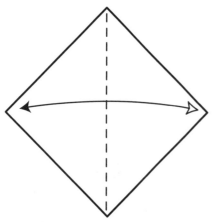

1. Start with a square paper.
Fold diagonally side to side
and unfold.

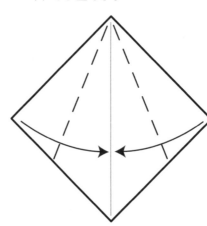

2. Fold sides to middle.

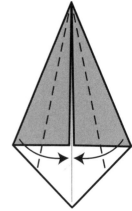

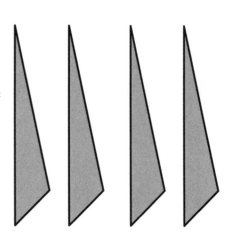

3. Fold sides to middle aga[in]

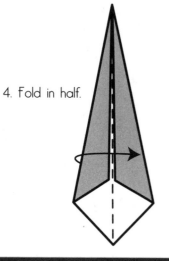

4. Fold in half.

5. Repeat steps 1-4 to make
a total of four pieces.

WHEAT PART I

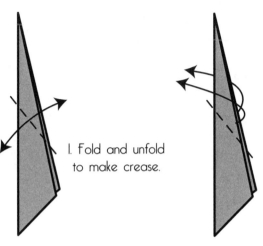

I. Fold and unfold
to make crease.

2. Open model slightly
and fold sides back.

3. Part I finished.

WHEAT PART 2

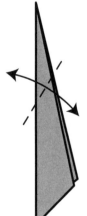

I. Fold and unfold
to make crease.

2. Fold sides forward to
make inside reverse fold.

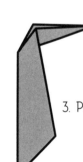

3. Part 2 finished.

WHEAT
and the Tares (continued)

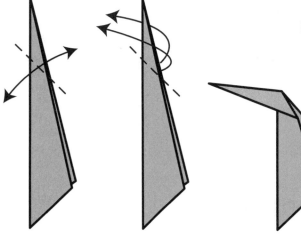

WHEAT PART 3

1. Fold and unfold to make crease. (Note: this crease is higher than the crease in part 1.)
2. Open model slightly and fold sides back.
3. Part 3 finished.

WHEAT PART 4

1. Leave fourth piece as is.

WHEAT ASSEMBLY

1. Layer four parts inside one another in order of 1, 3, 4, 2.

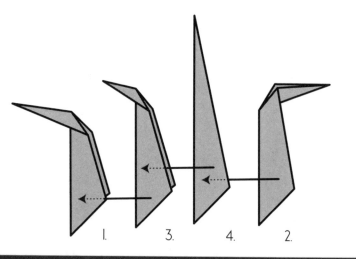

1.   3.   4.   2.

WHEAT ASSEMBLY
(continued)

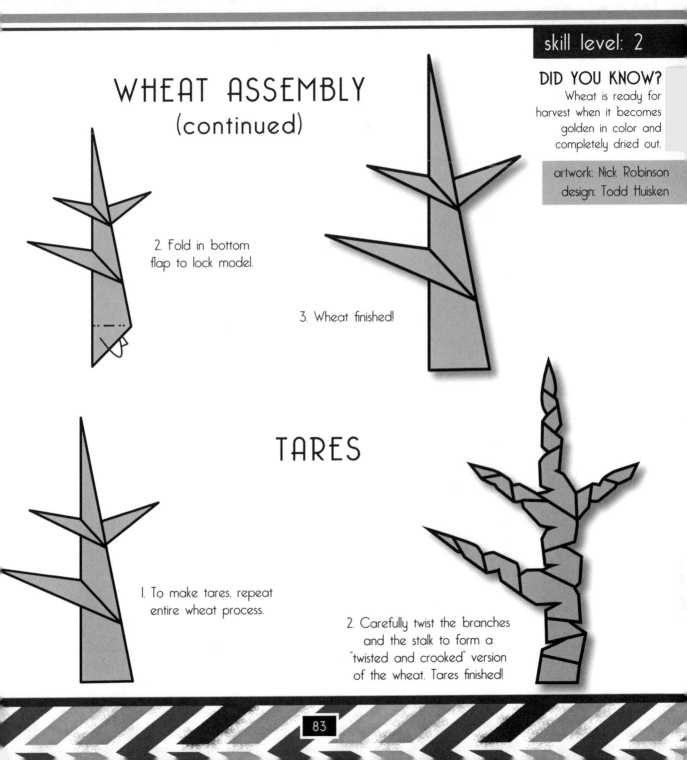

DID YOU KNOW?
Wheat is ready for harvest when it becomes golden in color and completely dried out.

artwork: Nick Robinson
design: Todd Huisken

2. Fold in bottom flap to lock model.

3. Wheat finished!

TARES

1. To make tares, repeat entire wheat process.

2. Carefully twist the branches and the stalk to form a "twisted and crooked" version of the wheat. Tares finished!

83

DID YOU KNOW?
A fig tree is a medium-sized tree that can reach ten to thirty feet in height.

Parable of the
FIG TREE

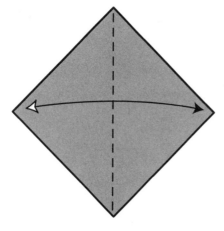

1. Fold in half diagonally and unfold.

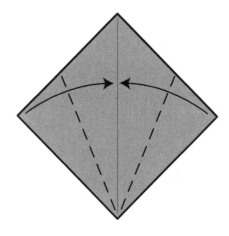

2. Fold sides into center.

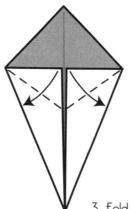

3. Fold flaps down.

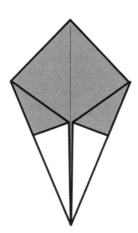

Turn model over

DID YOU KNOW?
Jesus once used the fig tree as an example of how to know when the second coming would occur. "Now learn a parable of the fig tree; When his branch is yet tender, and putteth forth leaves, ye know that summer is nigh: So likewise ye, when ye shall see all these things, know that it is near, even at the doors" (Matthew 24:32-33).

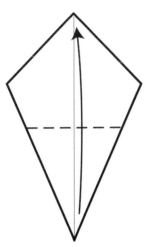

4. Fold bottom point up to top point.

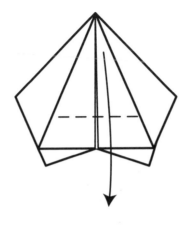

5. Fold top layer down.

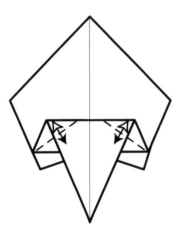

6. Fold and unfold flaps to prepare for steps 7 and 8.

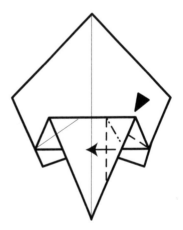

7. Fold right side over and squash flap flat.

Parable of the
FIG TREE
(continued)

DID YOU KNOW?
Figs have several health benefits: the fruit can be used in the treatment of chest congestion and as a facial mask that tightens the skin. Fig juice extracted from the leaves can be used to soothe insect bites.

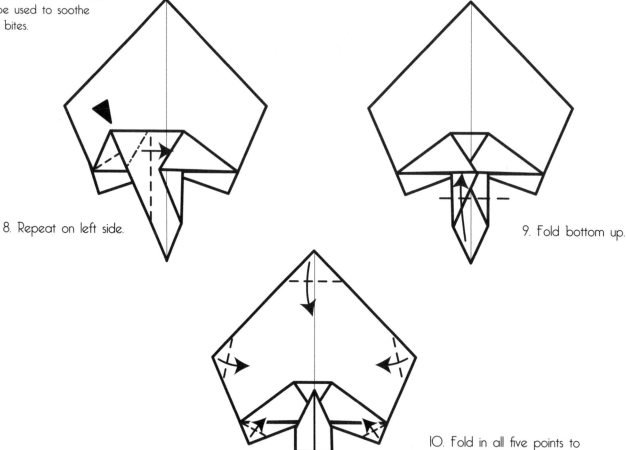

8. Repeat on left side.

9. Fold bottom up.

10. Fold in all five points to shape tree.

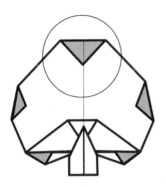

DID YOU KNOW?

Fig trees have no blossoms on their branches. The blossom is inside of the fruit! Many tiny flowers produce the little crunchy edible seeds that give figs their unique texture.

artwork: Nick Robinson
design: Todd Huisken

11. Fold top points in to further round the tree.

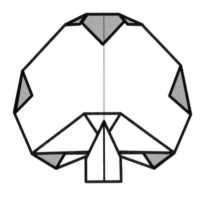

Turn model over.

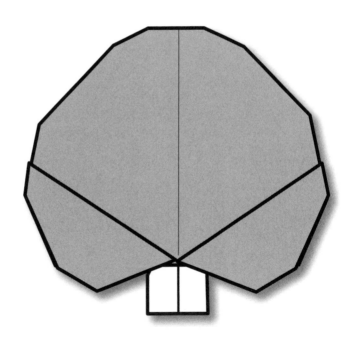

12. Fig tree finished!

INDEX
BY SKILL LEVEL

ABOUT THE AUTHOR

Todd Huisken is a licensed marriage and family therapist in Irvine, California. He has a bachelor's degree in psychology from Brigham Young University and a master's degree in marriage and family therapy from the University of San Diego. He has been in practice for twenty-one years. Todd has served as the assistant director of Disaster Mental Health Services for the Orange County chapter of the American Red Cross. He has worked with victims from the San Diego fires, Hurricanes Ivan and Katrina, and spent two weeks in Haiti following the earthquake in 2010. He is a writer, a runner, and a paper folder. Todd has been married to his beautiful wife for twenty-six years and they have three daughters and a son. In their free time, the Huiskens try to make Disneyland their second home.

Scan to visit

www.mormonorigami.com

0 26575 19608 5